For
Jean

POEMS, SONGS AND LETTERS BY
Robert Burns

FOR HIS WIFE,
Jean Armour

SELECTED AND INTRODUCED BY
Catherine Czerkawska

Published by Saraband
Suite 202, 98 Woodlands Road
Glasgow, G3 6HB
Scotland

www.saraband.net

ISBN: 9781910192436

Typeset by Iolaire Typography Ltd.
Printed and bound in Great Britain by Clays Ltd, St Ives plc.

1   3   5   7   9   10   8   6   4   2

Contents

Introduction

My novel *The Jewel* explores the dramatic relationship between Robert Burns and Jean Armour, the woman who, after a long and tempestuous courtship, finally became the poet's wife. Many biographers and critics have not been particularly kind to Jean. Burns's lover Margaret Campbell – or Highland Mary as she's more popularly known – was much more appealing to Victorian sensibilities as the demure heroine, conveniently dying young and depicted gazing adoringly up at her lover in a dozen Staffordshire flatbacks.

Similarly, the poet's overheated letters and beautiful poems to Nancy McLehose, aka 'Clarinda', are intriguingly mysterious. Did she succumb to the poet or not? Only the two people most closely involved could say for sure, and they never revealed the secret. Jean and Nancy did, however, take tea together some years after the poet's death, although I can't imagine that Nancy was moved to speak about the details of the relationship.

However, accounts of 'Jeanie' often range from dismissive to downright insulting. She has been called everything from 'glaikit' (foolish) to an unfeeling 'heifer'.

The best-known painted portraits of Jean Armour show an elderly woman, her strong face marked by ill health. There is a much more sympathetic picture of Jean as a widow, probably in her forties and very much at ease with herself, but what seems to be missing from most images and accounts is Jean's vitality. She was a vivacious brunette with a kindly manner, a steadfast generosity and a fine singing voice. Moreover, she had a fund of songs and melodies with which to enchant the lover who was to become her husband.

She may not have been scholarly, but she was certainly literate, as were her girlhood companions, the 'Mauchline belles', the self-consciously superior lassies of the town with their interest in fashion and novels. Later, her wisdom and strength of character in coping with her husband's infidelities, his moods, his illness and early death – not to mention the ever-present threat of poverty – speak to us of a woman of spirit and fortitude. And all while bringing up a family of children, including the poet's daughter by another woman.

Which of us would like to be defined by a couple of images of ourselves in our sixties after a hard life, bravely lived? Which of us would like to be judged, as Jean seems to have been by casual visitors to the Burns home, expecting the 'Bonnie Jean' of poetic imagination and finding a harassed wife with a newborn at the breast and a crowded household to run?

Nevertheless, Rab loved her, sometimes to the point of madness. He wrote poems and songs for and about her, occasionally changing her name when she had temporarily fallen out of his favour, as in 'Composed in Spring': 'And maun I still on Menie doat'. (There was no Menie, but there was certainly a Jeanie!) She was a lively and indomitable woman and although he occasionally shamed himself by damning his wife with faint praise to his gentry friends, his genuine affection for her never seems to have wavered. Nor did hers for him.

Until now there has been no single collection of the poems Robert Burns wrote with Jean Armour in mind, or at the very least with memories of their courtship informing the lyrics. Not all of the poems written for Jean are about the poet's wife. There were other lassies named Jean in his life and he said himself that he needed to be in love to write a love song. There is a kind of wilful determination about this and he went on having what can only be described as 'crushes' on young women throughout his life. I've taken a little latitude here and there, since some of the later songs must have reminded him of what he described as 'the honeymoon' – the first happy months of their marriage.

It will be clear to anyone reading these poems and songs – as well as the letters – that Rab and Jean's love for one another was real and abiding, even though they may occasionally have fallen out of liking.

What better way of describing their relationship than in the poet's own words:

'Till my last weary sand was run; till then—and then I love thee!'

Catherine Czerkawska

No. 19. *My heart was ance as blythe and free.*

Tune : *To the weaver's gin ye go.*   *Scots Musical Museum,* 1788, No. 103.

My heart was ance as blythe and free as sim-mer days were

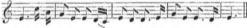

lang ; But a bonie, west-lin weaver lad Has gart me change my sang.

CHORUS.

To the weaver's gin ye go, fair maids, To the weaver's gin ye go, I rede you right, gang ne'er at night, To the weaver's gin ye go.

My heart was ance as blythe and free
As simmer days were lang ;
But a bonie, westlin weaver lad
Has gart me change my sang.

CHORUS.   *To the weaver's gin ye go, fair maids,*
To the weaver's gin ye go,
I rede you right, gang ne'er at night,
To the weaver's gin ye go.

My mither sent me to the town,
To warp a plaiden wab ;
But the weary, weary warpin o't
Has gart me sigh and sab.

A bonie, westlin weaver lad
Sat working at his loom ;
He took my heart, as wi' a net,
In every knot and thrum.

I sat beside my warpin-wheel,
And ay I ca'd it roun' ;
But every shot and every knock,
My heart it gae a stoun.

From: *The Songs of Robert Burns, A Study in Tone Poetry,*
James K Dick 1903.

Poems
and
Songs

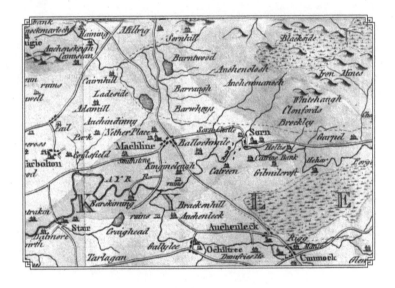

Map of Mauchline and surrounding countryside.

O Leave Novels

O leave novels, ye Mauchline belles,
Ye're safer at your spinning-wheel;
Such witching books are baited hooks
For rakish rooks, like Rob Mossgiel;
Your fine Tom Jones and Grandisons,
They make your youthful fancies reel;
They heat your brains, and fire your veins,
And then you're prey for Rob Mossgiel.

Beware a tongue that's smoothly hung,
A heart that warmly seems to feel;
That feeling heart but acts a part –
'Tis rakish art in Rob Mossgiel.
The frank address, the soft caress,
Are worse than poisoned darts of steel;
The frank address, and politesse,
Are all finesse in Rob Mossgiel.

The 'novels' of this poem are not a million miles from the stories that, some years later, fired the overactive imagination of Catherine Morland, the delightful heroine in Jane Austen's *Northanger Abbey*. Although it has often been assumed otherwise, the 'belles' of Mauchline were literate, and they would share popular novels, probably without the knowledge of disapproving parents who might well have been of the opinion that such things would heat their brains and fire their veins.

The poet (here named Mossgiel after the Burns family farm), like many young men, has a high opinion of himself as something of a rake. There are surviving accounts from those who knew him, describing an attractive young man, quite tall, spare, swarthy and strong: an idea romantic hero. Jean certainly thought so.

The Mauchline Lady

When first I came to Stewart Kyle,
My mind it was na steady;
Where'er I gaed, where'er I rade,
A mistress still I had aye.

But when I came roun' by Mauchline toun,
Not dreadin anybody,
My heart was caught, before I thought,
And by a Mauchline lady.

Tune: I Had a Horse, I Had Nae Mair

The 'Mauchline Lady' of the poem is, of course, Jean Armour, the first woman
really to capture the poet's heart.

The Belles of Mauchline

In Mauchline there dwells six proper young belles,
The pride of the place and its neighbourhood a',
Their carriage and dress, a stranger would guess,
 In Lon'on or Paris, they'd gotten it a'.

Miss Miller is fine, Miss Markland's divine,
Miss Smith she has wit, and Miss Betty is braw,
There's beauty and fortune to get wi' Miss Morton;
But Armour's the jewel for me o' them a'.

Tune: Bonie Dundee

The fashionable young ladies of Mauchline, flatteringly named in this song, are
sisters Helen and Betty Miller, Jean Markland, Jean Smith and Christina Morton,
whose father owned Morton's Ballroom, where Jean and Robert attended dancing
classes. Jean Armour, the daughter of a prosperous stonemason, was the 'jewel' of
them all, according to the poet.

My Heart Was Ance as Blithe and Free

My heart was ance as blithe and free
   As simmer days were lang,
But a bonnie, westlin' weaver lad
  Has gart me change my sang.

To the weavers gin ye go, fair maids,
   To the weavers gin ye go;
I rede you right gang ne'er at night,
   To the weavers gin ye go.

My mither sent me to the town,
   To warp a plaiden wab;
But the weary, weary warpin' o 't
   Has gart me sigh and sab.

To the weavers &c

A bonnie, westlin' weaver lad
   Sat working at his loom;
He took my heart as wi' a net,
   In every knot and thrum.

To the weavers &c

I sat beside my warpin-wheel,
    And aye I ca'd it roun';
But every shot and every knock,
    My heart it gae a stoun.

To the weavers &c

The moon was sinking in the west
    Wi' visage pale and wan,
As my bonnie westlin' weaver lad
    Convoy'd me thro' the glen.

To the weavers &c

But what was said, or what was done,
    Shame fa' me gin I tell;
But oh! I fear the kintra soon
    Will ken as weel's mysel'.

To the weavers &c

Tune: To The Weavers Gin Ye Go

The rhythm of this song cleverly echoes the movements and sounds of a loom. There is a story that Burns once asked a 'Mauchline Lady' to accompany him on a walk, but a local weaver got there first. Whether true or not, the song seems to be a light-hearted form of revenge on Jean's first suitor, a prosperous and God-fearing weaver called Rab Wilson, who was much preferred by her parents.

westlin': *from the west*
plaiden wab: *a length of woollen cloth*
sab: *sob*
stoun: *a leap*
kintra: *country*

For A' That

Tho' women's minds, like winter winds,
 May shift, and turn, an' a' that,
The noblest breast adores them maist –
 A consequence I draw that.

For a' that, an' a' that,
 And twice as meikle's a' that;
The bonie lass that I loe best
 She'll be my ain for a' that.

Great love I bear to a' the fair,
 Their humble slave, an' a' that;
But lordly will, I hold it still
 A mortal sin to thraw that.

For a' that, &c.

But there is ane aboon the lave,
 Has wit, and sense, an' a' that;
A bonie lass, I like her best,
 And wha a crime dare ca that?

For a' that, &c.

In rapture sweet this hour we meet,
    Wi' mutual love an' a' that,
But for how lang the flie may stang,
    Let inclination law that.

For a' that, &c.

Their tricks an' craft hae put me daft.
    They've taen me in, an' a' that;
But clear your decks, and here's-'The Sex!'
    I like the jads for a' that.

For a' that, &c.

Tune: For a' that

This is an earlier version of *A Man's a Man for a' That*, which is much better known.
It was written when Burns was still courting Jean in secret.

meikle: *much*
to thraw: *to thwart*
aboon the lave: *above the rest*
stang: *sting, nip*
jad: *hussy (often pejorative)*

There Was a Lass and She Was Fair

There was a lass, and she was fair,
At kirk or market to be seen;
When a' our fairest maids were met,
The fairest maid was bonie Jean.

And aye she wrought her mammie's wark,
And aye she sang sae merrilie;
The blythest bird upon the bush
Had ne'er a lighter heart than she.

But hawks will rob the tender joys
That bless the little lintwhite's nest;
And frost will blight the fairest flowers,
And love will break the soundest rest.

Young Robie was the brawest lad,
The flower and pride of a' the glen;
And he had owsen, sheep, and kye,
And wanton naigies nine or ten.

He gaed wi' Jeanie to the tryste,
He danc'd wi' Jeanie on the down;
And, lang ere witless Jeanie wist,
Her heart was tint, her peace was stown!

As in the bosom of the stream,
The moon-beam dwells at dewy e'en;
So trembling, pure, was tender love
Within the breast of bonie Jean.

And now she works her mammie's wark,
And aye she sighs wi' care and pain;
Yet wist na what her ail might be,
Or what wad make her weel again.

But did na Jeanie's heart loup light,
And didna joy blink in her e'e,
As Robie tauld a tale o' love
Ae e'ening on the lily lea?

The sun was sinking in the west,
The birds sang sweet in ilka grove;
His cheek to hers he fondly laid,
And whisper'd thus his tale o' love:

"O Jeanie fair, I lo'e thee dear;
O canst thou think to fancy me,
Or wilt thou leave thy mammie's cot,
And learn to tent the farms wi' me?

"At barn or byre thou shalt na drudge,
Or naething else to trouble thee;
But stray amang the heather-bells,
And tent the waving corn wi' me."

Now what could artless Jeanie do?
She had nae will to say him na:
At length she blush'd a sweet consent,
And love was aye between them twa.

Tune: Bonie Jean

Burns wrote to his friend George Thomson, the music publisher, that the heroine of this poem, written in 1793, was the daughter of one of the subscribers to a volume of Scots songs, rather than his wife. But since he also said that the 'air came from Mrs Burns's wood-note wild' we may assume that he told a different tale to Jean.

owsen: *oxen*
kye: *cattle*
naigies: *horses*
wist: *knew*
tint: *taken*
stown: *stolen*

Her Flowing Locks

Her flowing locks, the raven's wing,
Adown her neck and bosom hing;
How sweet unto that breast to cling,
And round that neck entwine her!

Her lips are roses wat wi' dew,
O what a feast her bonie mou'!
Her cheeks a mair celestial hue,
A crimson still diviner!

This is a fragment, a little later rewritten as *Farewell to Ballochmyle*. The description seems to fit Jean's dark-haired beauty very well.

wat: *wet*
mou': *mouth*

Tam Glen

My heart is a-breaking, dear Tittie,
Some counsel unto me come len',
To anger them a' is a pity,
But what will I do wi' Tam Glen?

I'm thinking wi' sic a braw fellow,
In poortith I might mak a fen;
What care I in riches to wallow,
If I maunna marry Tam Glen!

There's Lowrie the Laird o' Dumeller-
"Gude day to you, brute!" he comes ben:
He brags and he blaws o' his siller,
But when will he dance like Tam Glen!

My minnie does constantly deave me,
And bids me beware o' young men;
They flatter, she says, to deceive me,
But wha can think sae o' Tam Glen!

My daddie says, gin I'll forsake him,
He'd gie me gude hundermarks ten;
But, if it's ordain'd I maun take him,
O wha will I get but Tam Glen!

Yestreen at the Valentine's dealing,
My heart to my mou' gied a sten';
For thrice I drew ane without failing,
And thrice it was written 'Tam Glen'!

The last Halloween I was waukin
My droukit sark-sleeve, as ye ken,
His likeness came up the house staukin,
And the very grey breeks o' Tam Glen!

Come, counsel, dear Tittie, don't tarry;
I'll gie ye my bonie black hen,
Gif ye will advise me to marry
The lad I lo'e dearly, Tam Glen.

Tune: The Merry Beggars

Although the lover in this song is called Tam Glen, and it was written long after Robert and Jean were married, the theme of marrying for love rather than riches is one that the poet returned to time and again, especially where his relationship with Jean was concerned.

It is fascinating for the insight it gives us into the lowland Scots Valentine and Hallowe'en customs of the time, which we know that both Robert and Jean indulged in during the years of their courtship.

braw: *handsome*
poortith: *poverty*
mak a fen: *maintain myself*
minnie: *mother*
to my mou' gied a sten': *jumped into my mouth*
waukin: *keeping watch over*
wroukit: *drenched*
sark-sleeve: *shirt sleeve (this refers to the custom of hanging a wet shirt sleeve before the fire and
        then watching it dry, whereupon the likeness of the woman's future husband will appear)*
breeks: *breeches*

I'll Ay Ca' in by Yon Town

I'll aye ca' in by yon town,
And by yon garden green again;
I'll aye ca' in by yon town,
And see my bonie Jean again.

There's nane sall ken, there's nane can guess
What brings me back the gate again,
But she, my fairest, faithfu' lass,
And stownlins we sall meet again.

I'll aye ca' in, &c

She'll wander by the aiken tree,
When trystin time draws near again;
And when her lovely form I see,
O haith! she's doubly dear again.

I'll aye ca' in &c

Tune: I'll Gang Nae Mair To Yon Toun

This is another song that, although dated some years after the event, recalls the secret meetings between Robert and Jean, when Jean's parents disapproved of the poet. Certainly, even while Robert was in Edinburgh and was writing love letters to Nancy McLehose, he was still arranging the occasional 'tryst' with Jean: he could never quite keep away.

The town of the song is presumably Mauchline and we know that the couple were in the habit of meeting in the countryside round about. It may be that for Robert, the 'garden green' is the garden of Netherplace House on the edge of the town.

stownlins: *in a secretive manner*
aiken: *oak*
trystin: *meeting or assignation*
O haith!: *exclamation of surprise*

O Whistle, and I'll Come to You, My Lad

O whistle, and I'll come to you, my lad,
O whistle, and I'll come to you, my lad:
Tho' father and mither and a' should gae mad,
Thy Jeanie will venture wi' ye my lad.

But warily tent, when you come to court me,
And come na unless the back-yett be a-jee;
Syne up the back-stile and let naebody see,
And come as ye were na comin' to me.
And come as ye were na comin' to me.

At kirk, or at market, whene'er ye meet me,
Gang by me as tho' that ye car'd na a flie;
But steal me a blink o' your bonnie black e'e,
Yet look as ye were na lookin' at me.
Yet look as ye were na lookin' at me.

Ay vow and protest that ye care na for me,
And whiles ye may lightly my beauty a wee;
But court na anither, tho' jokin' ye be,
For fear that she wyle your fancy frae me.
For fear that she wyle your fancy frae me.

O whistle, and I'll come to you, my lad,
O whistle, and I'll come to you, my lad:
Tho' father and mither and a' should gae mad,
Thy Jeanie will venture wi' ye, my lad.

Tune: John Bruce's Air

This song, a reworking of a traditional version, was said to be a favourite with Jean and seems to describe her and Robert's courtship very accurately, especially during the many months when they were meeting in secret. Her father and mother certainly did 'gae mad' when they learned of the liaison. In fact, her father fainted clean away.

The song clearly meant a great deal to her, even later in what had become a somewhat troubled marriage. Two years after first writing it, the poet changed the fourth line to 'Thy Jeanie will venture wi' ye, my lad' on the instructions of his wife, or so he told George Thomson, for whom he was collecting songs:

'A fair dame at whose shrine I, the priest of the Nine, offer up the incense of Parnassus; a dame whom the graces had attired in witchcraft and whom the Loves have armed with lightning; a fair one, herself the heroine of the song, insists on the amendment, and dispute her commands if you dare.'

Beneath the overblown sentiments is one of several references to Jean Armour as his muse, a fact routinely ignored, just as 'Jean's version' of the song has been sadly neglected in subsequent renderings.

tent: *pay attention, heed*
back-yett: *back gate*
a-jee: *ajar*
back-stile: *back stair*

This Is No My Ain Lassie

This is no my ain lassie,
Fair tho' the lassie be:
Weel ken I my ain lassie,
Kind love is in her e'e.

I see a form, I see a face,
Ye weel may wi' the fairest place:
It wants, to me, the witching grace,
The kind love that's in her e'e.

This is no &c.

She 's bonie, blooming, straight and tall;
And lang has had my heart in thrall;
And ay it charms my very saul,
The kind love that 's in her e'e.

O this is no &c.

A thief sae pawkie is my Jean
To steal a blink by a' unseen;
But gleg as light are lover's een,
When kind love is in the e'e.

O this is no &c.

It may escape the courtly sparks,
It may escape the learned clerks;
But well the watching lover marks
The kind love that 's in her e'e.

O this is no &c.

Tune: This Is No My Ain House

This song speaks of a longstanding affection for Jean, and Burns was always keen to stress his wife's kindness. The couple had spent many months of illicit courtship evading the unwelcome attentions of Jean's parents and the Mauchline kirk session, in the person of Holy Willie Fisher. There must have been times when 'stealing a blink by a' unseen' was the most that they could manage.

pawkie: *tricky*
gleg: *adroit*

'O Whistle and I'll Come to You, My Lad':
Illustration from Allan Cunningham's
Complete Works of Robert Burns, 1855.

I Reign in Jeanie's Bosom

Louis, what reck I by thee,
Or Geordie on his ocean?
Dyvor, beggar louns to me,
I reign in Jeanie's bosom!

Let her crown my love her law,
And in her breast enthrone me,
Kings and nations – swith awa'!
Reif randies, I disown ye!

Burns's poem for and about Jean so often have a certain energy about them that he tends to reserve for her alone. In this case, there's also a lovely, boastful sense of elation. Louis was still enthroned in France, King George was still ruling the waves – but nothing could compare to the way Robert felt as the king of 'Jeanie's bosom'.

reck: *think, consider*
dyvor: *bankrupt*
louns: *rascals*
swith: *off, away!*
reif randies: *thieves (abusive)*

Ye Hae Lien Wrang, Lassie

Your rosy cheeks are turned sae wan,
Ye're greener than the grass, lassie,
Your coatie's shorter by a span,
Yet deil an inch the less, lassie.

Ye hae lien wrang, lassie,
Ye've lien a' wrang,
Ye've lien in some unco bed,
An wi some unco man.

Ye've loot the pownie ower the dyke,
An he's been in the corn, lassie;
For ay the brose ye sup at e'en,
Ye bock them or the morn, lassie.

Ye hae lien wrang, lassie, &c

Fou lichtly lap ye ower the knowe,
An throu the wud ye sang, lassie
But herryin o the foggie byke,
I fear ye've got a stang, lassie.

Ye hae lien wrang, lassie, &c

Tune: Up and Waur Them A' Willie

From the poet's *Merrie Muses* collection of bawdy verse, this poem seems peculiarly well suited to Jean's predicament when she fell pregnant. It's a robust description of the dangers of lying in a strange bed with a strange man, with sexual intercourse described in terms of 'letting the pony across the ditch' and conception as a bee sting: twice, in Jean Armour's case, before the marriage was legitimised.

wan: *pale*
coatie: *short coat, top*
span: *hand's breadth*
deil an inch: *devil an inch*
lien: *lain*
unco: *strange*
loot: *let*
pownie: *pony*
dyke: *ditch*
brose: *form of porridge*
bock: *vomit*
lap: *leapt*
foggie byke: *bees' nest*
stang: *sting*

Here's His Health in Water

Altho' my back be at the wa',
And tho' he be the fautor;
Altho' my back be at the wa',
Yet, here's his health in water.

O wae gae by his wanton sides,
Sae brawlie's he could flatter;
Till for his sake I'm slighted sair,
And dree the kintra clatter.

But tho' my back be at the wa',
And tho' he be the fautor;
But tho' my back be at the wa',
Yet here's his health in water!

Tune: The Job of Journey-work

Dated 1786, when the troubles between Robert and Jean were at their worst, this braggardly verse – in which the poet assumes (rightly) that although he is the 'fautor' (culprit), he is still loved – was surely composed with Jean in mind.

fautor: *culprit*
brawlie's: *beautifully as*
dree: *bear, endure*
kintra: *country*
clatter: *gossip*

Portrait of Robert Burns,
after Alexander Nasmyth (1767).

The Posie

O luve will venture in where it daur na weel be seen,
O luve will venture in where wisdom ance has been;
But I will doun yon river rove, amang the wood sae
    green,
And a' to pu' a Posie to my ain dear May.

The primrose I will pu', the firstling o' the year,
And I will pu' the pink, the emblem o' my dear;
For she's the pink o' womankind, and blooms without
a
    peer,
And a' to be a Posie to my ain dear May.

I'll pu' the budding rose, when Phoebus peeps in view,
For it's like a baumy kiss o' her sweet, bonie mou;
The hyacinth's for constancy wi' its unchanging blue,
And a' to be a Posie to my ain dear May.

The lily it is pure, and the lily it is fair,
And in her lovely bosom I'll place the lily there;
The daisy's for simplicity and unaffected air,
And a' to be a Posie to my ain dear May.

The hawthorn I will pu', wi' its locks o' siller gray,
Where, like an aged man, it stands at break o' day;
But the songster's nest within the bush

I winna tak away
And a' to be a Posie to my ain dear May.

The woodbine I will pu', when the e'ening star is near,
And the diamond draps o' dew shall be her een sae
    clear;
The violet's for modesty, which weel she fa's to wear,
And a' to be a Posie to my ain dear May.

I'll tie the Posie round wi' the silken band o' luve,
And I'll place it in her breast, and I'll
swear by a' above,
That to my latest draught o' life the band shall ne'er
    remove,
And this will be a Posie to my ain dear May.

Tune: The Posie

Burns wrote that this was his own composition, but the 'air was taken down from Mrs Burns's voice'. This may help to confirm our suspicions that the song was originally intended for his 'ain dear Jean' but was changed to 'May' during those months when Jeanie was out of favour and Highland Mary's star was in the ascendant.

baumy: *balmy*
mou: *mouth*
draps: *drops*

Gavin Hamilton's House, Mauchline,
with spring dancers on the green.

Tho' Cruel Fate Should Bid Us Part

Tho' cruel fate should bid us part,
    Far as the pole and line,
Her dear idea round my heart,
    Should tenderly entwine.
Tho' mountains, rise, and deserts howl,
    And oceans roar between;
Yet, dearer than my deathless soul,
    I still would love my Jean.

Tune: The Northern Lass

Written in 1785, at a time when the relationship between Jean and Robert was stormy, mostly because of parental disapproval, this fragment plays around with ideas that are found elsewhere in the poet's songs and poems for his wife.

The Banks o' Doon

Ye flowery banks o' bonie Doon,
    How can ye blume sae fair?
How can ye chant, ye little birds,
     And I sae fu' o care!
Thou'll break my heart, thou bonie bird,
    That sings upon the bough!
Thou minds me o' the happy days
    When my fause Luve was true.
Thou'll break my heart, thou bonie bird,
    That sings beside thy mate;
For sae I sat, and sae I sang,
    And wist na o' my fate.

Aft hae I rov'd by bonie Doon,
    To see the woodbine twine;
And ilka bird sang o' its Luve,
     And sae did I o' mine.
Wi' lightsome heart I pu'd a rose,
     Upon its thorny tree;
But my fause Luver staw my rose,
    And left the thorn wi' me.
Wi' lightsome heart I pu'd a rose,
    Upon a morn in June;
And sae I flourished on the morn,
    And sae was pu'd or noon.

Tune: Caledonian Hunt's Delight

This is another song that was collected and rewritten by Burns. There are three versions, of which this is the second, and perhaps the one that might be most closely associated with Jean. In this version the young woman is very definitely compared to a bird, singing in blissful ignorance of the unwelcome consequences of her love. (Robert frequently characterised Jean as a songbird.) The poet was certainly adept at sympathising with a young woman faced with the consequences of an unwise attachment.

Song Composed in August

Now westlin winds and slaught'ring guns
Bring Autumn's pleasant weather;
The moorcock springs on whirring wings
Amang the blooming heather:
Now waving grain, wide o'er the plain,
Delights the weary farmer;
And the moon shines bright, when I rove at night,
To muse upon my charmer.

The partridge loves the fruitful fells,
The plover loves the mountains;
The woodcock haunts the lonely dells,
The soaring hern the fountains:
Thro' lofty groves the cushat roves,
The path of man to shun it;
The hazel bush o'erhangs the thrush,
The spreading thorn the linnet.

Thus ev'ry kind their pleasure find,
The savage and the tender;
Some social join, and leagues combine,
Some solitary wander:
Avaunt, away! the cruel sway,
Tyrannic man's dominion;
The sportsman's joy, the murd'ring cry,
The flutt'ring, gory pinion!

But, Peggy dear, the ev'ning's clear,
Thick flies the skimming swallow,
The sky is blue, the fields in view,
All fading-green and yellow:
Come let us stray our gladsome way,
And view the charms of Nature;
The rustling corn, the fruited thorn,
And ev'ry happy creature.

We'll gently walk, and sweetly talk,
Till the silent moon shine clearly;
I'll grasp thy waist, and, fondly prest,
Swear how I love thee dearly:
Not vernal show'rs to budding flow'rs,
Not Autumn to the farmer,
So dear can be as thou to me,
My fair, my lovely charmer!

Tune: I Had a Horse, I Had Nae Mair

There is some evidence that this song was originally written for Jean Armour, but the poet – never one to waste a good love lyric – substituted 'Peggy' for 'Jeanie' when he was feeling something less than enchanted with Jean. It's interesting to note that Armour can be substituted for charmer and that Highland Mary's real name was the Gaelic form of Margaret or Peggy. Robert's relationship with his Highland lass was intense but shortlived, at a time when he was feeling particularly disgruntled with Jean.

cushat: *wood pigeon, ring dove*

Composed in Spring

Again rejoicing nature sees
Her robe assume its vernal hues,
Her leafy looks wave in the breeze,
All freshly steep'd in morning dews.

And maun I still on Menie doat,
And bear the scorn that's in her ee?
For it's jet, jet black, an' it's like a hawk,
An' it winna let a body be!

In vain to me the cowslips blaw,
In vain to me the vi'lets spring;
In vain to me, in glen or shaw,
The mavis and the lintwhite sing.

And maun I still &c

The merry ploughboy cheers his team,
Wi' joy the tentie seedsman stalks,
But life to me 's a weary dream,
A dream of ane that never wauks.

And maun I still &c

The wanton coot the water skims,
Among the reeds the ducklings cry,
The stately swan majestic swims,
And every thing is blest but I.

And maun I still &c

The shepherd steeks his faulding slap,
And owre the moorlands whistles shill,
Wi' wild, unequal, wand'ring step,
I meet him on the dewy hill.

And maun I still &c

And when the lark, 'tween light and dark,
Blythe waukens by the daisy's side,
And mounts and sings on fluttering wings,
A woe-worn ghaist I hameward glide.

And maun I still &c

Come, Winter, with thine angry howl,
And raging bend the naked tree;
Thy gloom will soothe my cheerless soul,
When Nature all is sad like me!

And maun I still &c

Tune: Jockey's Grey Breeks

This was written in 1786 when the poet was in mental turmoil about his relationship with Jean, believing that she had rejected him under pressure from her parents. He wrote that he was 'nine parts and nine tenths out of ten stark staring mad'. No other woman ever seemed to inspire such passion in him. He changed the name Jeanie to Menie in this poem, in a not very successful attempt to disguise his feelings. In every chorus, he fancies that Jean Armour's dark eyes – here likened to the pitiless eyes of a hawk – are gazing at him with scorn. Poor Jean was beleaguered: pregnant with Robert's twins, bullied by her parents, and now berated by the man she loved. This is one of two poems that read like a prolonged howl of despair and rage.

vernal: *green*
maun: *must*
mavis: *song thrush*
lintwhite: *linnet*
tentie: *attentive*
steeks his faulding slap: *shuts up or fastens his entrance gate*
ghaist: *ghost*

Ellisland, engraving.

Lament

O thou pale orb that silent shines
While care-untroubled mortals sleep!
Thou seest a wretch who inly pines,
And wanders here to wail and weep!
With woe I nightly vigils keep,
Beneath thy wan, unwarming beam;
And mourn, in lamentation deep,
How life and love are all a dream!

I joyless view thy rays adorn
The faintly-marked, distant hill;
I joyless view thy trembling horn,
Reflected in the gurgling rill:
My fondly-fluttering heart, be still!
Thou busy pow'r, remembrance, cease!
Ah! must the agonizing thrill
For ever bar returning peace!

No idly-feign'd, poetic pains,
My sad, love-lorn lamentings claim:
No shepherd's pipe - Arcadian strains;
No fabled tortures, quaint and tame.
The plighted faith, the mutual flame,
The oft-attested pow'rs above,
The promis'd father's tender name;
These were the pledges of my love!

Encircled in her clasping arms,
How have the raptur'd moments flown!
How have I wish'd for fortune's charms,
For her dear sake, and her's alone!
And, must I think it! is she gone,
My secret heart's exulting boast?
And does she heedless hear my groan?
And is she ever, ever lost?

Oh! can she bear so base a heart,
So lost to honour, lost to truth,
As from the fondest lover part,
The plighted husband of her youth?
Alas! life's path may be unsmooth!
Her way may lie thro' rough distress!
Then, who her pangs and pains will soothe
Her sorrows share, and make them less?

Ye winged hours that o'er us pass'd,
Enraptur'd more, the more enjoy'd,
Your dear remembrance in my breast
My fondly-treasur'd thoughts employ'd:
That breast, how dreary now, and void,
For her too scanty once of room!
Ev'n ev'ry ray of hope destroy'd,
And not a wish to gild the gloom!

The morn, that warns th' approaching day,
Awakes me up to toil and woe;
I see the hours in long array,

That I must suffer, lingering, slow:
Full many a pang, and many a throe,
Keen recollection's direful train,
Must wring my soul, ere Phoebus, low,
Shall kiss the distant western main.

And when my nightly couch I try,
Sore harass'd out with care and grief,
My toil-beat nerves, and tear-worn eye,
Keep watchings with the nightly thief:
Or if I slumber, fancy, chief,
Reigns, haggard-wild, in sore affright:
Ev'n day, all-bitter, brings relief
From such a horror-breathing night.

O thou bright queen, who o'er th' expanse
Now highest reign'st, with boundless sway
Oft has thy silent-marking glance
Observ'd us, fondly-wand'ring, stray!
The time, unheeded, sped away,
While love's luxurious pulse beat high,
Beneath thy silver-gleaming ray,
To mark the mutual-kindling eye.

Oh! scenes in strong remembrance set!
Scenes, never, never to return!
Scenes, if in stupor I forget,
Again I feel, again I burn!
From ev'ry joy and pleasure torn,
Life's weary vale I'll wander thro';
And hopeless, comfortless, I'll mourn
A faithless woman's broken vow!

This relentlessly self-dramatising but passionate piece of work was published in Burns's first collection – the famous Kilmarnock edition. Jean, pregnant with the poet's first set of twins, read it and must have recognised herself as the 'faithless woman', but perhaps that was the writer's intention: an early example of 'revenge poetry', in which Burns would prove to be very skilled. Nevertheless, a real sense of hurt and a genuinely abiding love manage to shine through the over-heated verses. Goodness knows what poor Jean made of it all.

Farewell Song to the Banks of Ayr

The gloomy night is gath'ring fast,
Loud roars the wild, inconstant blast,
Yon murky cloud is foul with rain,
I see it driving o'er the plain;
The hunter now has left the moor.
The scatt'red coveys meet secure;
While here I wander, prest with care,
Along the lonely banks of Ayr.

The Autumn mourns her rip'ning corn
By early Winter's ravage torn;
Across her placid, azure sky,
She sees the scowling tempest fly:
Chill runs my blood to hear it rave;
I think upon the stormy wave,
Where many a danger I must dare,
Far from the bonie banks of Ayr.

'Tis not the surging billow's roar,
'Tis not that fatal, deadly shore;
Tho' death in ev'ry shape appear,
The wretched have no more to fear:
But round my heart the ties are bound,
That heart transpierc'd with many a wound;
These bleed afresh, those ties I tear,
To leave the bonie banks of Ayr.

Farewell, old Coila's hills and dales,
Her healthy moors and winding vales;
The scenes where wretched Fancy roves,
Pursuing past, unhappy loves!
Farewell, my friends! farewell, my foes!
My peace with these, my love with those:
The bursting tears my heart declare-
Farewell, the bonie banks of Ayr!

Written at a time when the poet was planning to leave for Jamaica – chief among
his 'past unhappy loves' was, of course, Jean Armour.

It Is Na, Jean, Thy Bonie Face

It is na, Jean, thy bonie face,
Nor shape that I admire;
Altho' thy beauty and thy grace
Might weel awauk desire.

Something, in ilka part o thee,
To praise, to love, I find,
But dear as is thy form to me,
Still dearer is thy mind.

Nae mair ungenerous wish I hae,
Nor stronger in my breast,
Than, if I canna make thee sae,
At least to see thee blest.

Content am I, if heaven shall give
But happiness, to thee;
And as wi' thee I'd wish to live,
For thee I'd bear to die.

Tune: The Maid's Complaint

---

awauk: *awake*
ilka: *every*

I Hae a Wife of My Ain

I Hae a wife of my ain,
I'll partake wi naebody;
I'll take Cuckold frae nane,
I'll gie Cuckold to naebody.

I hae a penny to spend,
There-thanks to naebody!
I hae naething to lend,
I'll borrow frae naebody.

I am naebody's lord,
I'll be slave to naebody;
I hae a gude braid sword,
I'll tak dunts frae naebody.

I'll be merry and free,
I'll be sad for naebody;
Naebody cares for me,
I care for naebody.

Tune: I Hae a Wife of My Ain

There is something wonderfully exuberant and celebratory about this poem,
written when Jean and Robert were finally, officially married.

braid: *broad*
dunts: *blows*

My Wife's a Winsome Wee Thing

She is a winsome wee thing,
She is a handsome wee thing,
She is a lo'esome wee thing,
This dear wife o' mine.

I never saw a fairer,
I never lo'ed a dearer,
And neist my heart I'll wear her,
For fear my jewel tine,

She is a winsome, &c.

The warld's wrack we share o't;
The warstle and the care o't;
Wi' her I'll blythely bear it,
And think my lot divine.

She is a winsome, &c.

Tune: My Wife's a Wanton Wee Thing

---

winsome: *pleasing or attractive*
tine: *tarnish*
wrack: *destruction, difficulty*
warstle: *struggle*

Of A' the Airts

Of a' the airts the wind can blaw,
I dearly like the west,
For there the bonnie lassie lives,
The lassie I lo'e best:
There wild-woods grow, and rivers row,
And mony a hill between;
But day and night my fancy's flight
Is ever wi' my Jean.

I see her in the dewy flowers,
I see her sweet and fair:
I hear her in the tunefu' birds,
I hear her charm the air:
There's not a bonnie flower that springs
By fountain, shaw, or green,
There's not a bonnie bird that sings,
But minds me o' my Jean.

Tune: Miss Admiral Gordon's Strathspey

Burns himself said that this was written 'during the honeymoon'. The song is nonetheless powerful for its simplicity. Whenever the poet uses the word 'clean' in this context, it has a sense of 'shapely' or 'well formed'. It is also interesting to note that Burns frequently refers to birdsong in reference to his wife, who he said had the 'finest wood-note wild in the country'.

blaw: *blow*
shaw: *copse*

O, Were I on Parnassus Hill

O, were I on Parnassus hill,
Or had o' Helicon my fill,
That I might catch poetic skill,
To sing how dear I love thee!
But Nith maun be my Muse's well,
My Muse maun be thy bonie sel',
On Corsincon I'll glowr and spell,
And write how dear I love thee.

Then come, sweet Muse, inspire my lay!
For a' the lee-lang simmer's day
I couldna sing, I couldna say,
How much, how dear, I love thee,
I see thee dancing o'er the green,
Thy waist sae jimp, thy limbs sae clean,
Thy tempting lips, thy roguish een—
By Heaven and Earth I love thee!

By night, by day, a-field, at hame,
The thoughts o' thee my breast inflame:
And aye I muse and sing thy name—
I only live to love thee.
Tho' I were doom'd to wander on,
Beyond the sea, beyond the sun,
Till my last weary sand was run;
Till then—and then I love thee!

Tune: My Love Is Lost To Me

According to Robert, this song 'was made out of compliment to Mrs Burns'. In fact, he was overseeing the building of his new Ellisland farmhouse down in Dumfriesshire, while Jean was living in Mauchline and walking out to Mossgiel each day, to learn about dairying and to visit her little son, Robbie. Living in lodgings that could only be described as a hovel, and missing Jean, the poet would travel back and forth on horseback between Ellisland and Mauchline more frequently than was advisable, given the amount of work he had to do. When he could see Corsincon Hill, near Cumnock, he knew that he would soon be home. His young wife would often walk out along the road to meet him. Parnassus Hill was the home of the Muses in Greek mythology, and it is clear that he saw Jean as his own 'sweet Muse'. There is a profound sensuality about these lines, coupled with a certainty of permanence (however improbable) that anyone who has ever been deeply in love will surely recognise.

spell: *tell tales, exaggerate a little*
lay: *poem*
lee-lang: *long*
jimp: *slender, dainty*
clean: *clean-cut*
een: *eyes*

Lady Mary Ann

O lady Mary Ann looks o'er the Castle wa',
She saw three bonie boys playing at the ba',
The youngest he was the flower amang them a',
My bonie laddie's young, but he's growin' yet.

O father, O father, an ye think it fit,
We'll send him a year to the college yet,
We'll sew a green ribbon round about his hat,
And that will let them ken he's to marry yet.

Lady Mary Ann was a flower in the dew,
Sweet was its smell and bonie was its hue,
And the longer it blossom'd the sweeter it grew,
For the lily in the bud will be bonier yet.

Young Charlie Cochran was the sprout of an aik,
Bonie and bloomin' and straught was its make,
The sun took delight to shine for its sake,
And it will be the brag o' the forest yet.

The simmer is gane when the leaves they were green,
And the days are awa' that we hae seen,
But far better days I trust will come again;
For my bonie laddie's young, but he's growin' yet.

Tune: Craigton's Growing

This song, not directly written for Jean, may nevertheless have been a favourite with her. The words are based on a traditional ballad collected by David Herd, in which a young woman is betrothed to a mere boy, whom she must wait to wed. Whereupon, in traditional ballad manner, he is dead and gone by the age of eighteen. In Burns's skilled hands, while still retaining the mysterious flavour of all ancient ballads, it seems to have been transformed into a song that is as much about a mother's love for her sons as it is about a longing for a husband, and therefore seems a fitting addition to a collection of poems and songs for Jean.

aik: *oak*

The Lea Rig

When o'er the hill the eastern star
Tells bughtin time is near, my jo,
And owsen frae the furrow'd field
Return sae dowf and weary O;
Down by the burn, where birken buds
Wi' dew are hangin clear, my jo,
I'll meet thee on the lea-rig,
My ain kind Dearie O.

At midnight hour, in mirkest glen,
I'd rove, and ne'er be eerie, O,
If thro' that glen I gaed to thee,
My ain kind Dearie O;
Altho' the night were ne'er sae wild,
And I were ne'er sae weary O,
I'll meet thee on the lea-rig,
My ain kind Dearie O.

The hunter lo'es the morning sun;
To rouse the mountain deer, my jo;
At noon the fisher seeks the glen
Adown the burn to steer, my jo:
Gie me the hour o' gloamin' grey,
It maks my heart sae cheery O,
To meet thee on the lea-rig,
My ain kind Dearie O.

Tune: The Lea Rig

This is an old song, collected and shaped by Burns into a very beautiful lyric. It is one I have always associated with Jean and seems to describe something of their life together at Ellisland, when (for at least some of the time) the couple would have been working together in the way described. The poet was very insistent that the 'air' should not be changed in any way.

bughtin: *gathering sheep into the fold*
owsen: *oxen*
dowf: *dull*
lea-rig: *fallow ridge of land*
eerie: *fearful*

Ca' the Yowes

Ca' the yowes to the knowes,
Ca' them where the heather grows,
Ca' them where the burnie rowes,
My bonie Dearie

Hark the mavis' e'ening sang,
Sounding Clouden's woods amang;
Then a-faulding let us gang,
My bonie Dearie.

Ca' the yowes, &c.

We'll gae down by Clouden side,
Thro' the hazels, spreading wide,
O'er the waves that sweetly glide,
To the moon sae clearly.

Ca' the yowes, &c.

Yonder Clouden's silent towers,
Where, at moonshine's midnight hours,
O'er the dewy-bending flowers,
Fairies dance sae cheery.

Ca' the yowes, &c.

Ghaist nor bogle shalt thou fear,
Thou'rt to Love and Heav'n sae dear,
Nocht of ill may come thee near;
My bonie Dearie.

Ca' the yowes, &c.

Fair and lovely as thou art,
Thou hast stown my very heart;
I can die - but canna part,
My bonie Dearie.

Ca' the yowes, &c.

Tune: Ca' the Yowes

There are several versions of this song, of which this is perhaps the best known.
Once again, it seems to describe that happy time when the poet and his wife were
working together at Ellisland on the River Nith, before ill health, marital discord
and the threat of poverty all conspired to generate domestic discord.

yowes: *ewes*
burnie: *burn*
a-fauldin: *putting the sheep into the fold*
Clouden: *Lincluden Priory*
ghaist: *ghost*
bogle: *bogeyman*
stown: *stolen*

Country Lassie

In simmer, when the hay was mawn,
And corn wav'd green in ilka field,
While claver blooms white o'er the lea,
And roses blaw in ilka bield;
Blithe Bessie in the milking shiel,
Says, I'll be wed, come o't what will;
Out spak a dame in wrinkled eild,
O' guid advisement comes nae ill.
It's ye hae wooers mony ane,
And, lassie, ye're but young ye ken;
Then wait a wee, and cannie wale,
A routhie butt, a routhie ben:
There's Johnie o' the Buskie-glen,
Fu' is his barn, fu' is his byre;
Tak this frae me, my bonnie hen,
It's plenty beats the luver's fire.

For Johnie o' the Buskie-glen,
I dinna care a single flie;
He lo'es sae weel his craps and kye,
He has nae luve to spare for me:
But blithe's the blink o' Robie's e'e,
And weel I wat he lo'es me dear:
Ae blink o' him I wad nae gie
For Buskie-glen and a' his gear.

O thoughtless lassie, life's a faught;
The canniest gate, the strife is sair;
But ay fu' han't is fechtin best,
An hungry care's an unco care:
But some will spend, and some will spare,
An' wilfu' folk maun hae their will;
Syne as ye brew, my maiden fair,
Keep mind that ye maun drink the yill.

O, gear will buy me rigs o' land,
And gear will buy me sheep and kye
But the tender heart o' leesome luve,
The gowd and siller canna buy;
We may be poor, Robie and I,
Light is the burden luve lays on;
Content and luve brings peace and joy,
What mair hae queens upon a throne?

Tune: The Country Lass or Sally In Our Alley

Although the 'country lassie' of this song is named Bessie rather than Jean – and might well have been Betsy Paton, who bore Rab his first child – it is clear that the poet never had any intention of marrying Betsy, much as his mother might have wished it. The tricky but intensely beautiful melody is one that would have suited Jean's voice; while the circumstances of the song, in which an older woman counsels caution to an innocent lassie who wants to marry her 'Robie' in spite of an offer from a much wealthier man, are reminiscent of Jean and Rab's courtship. For me, there is something deeply moving about the dialogue, at once realistic and poetic, between the young and old women, each one right in her own way. This is Burns at his best: subtle, imaginative, sympathetic. And it would be true to say that Jean did indeed 'drink the yill' of her own brewing, however much she may have loved her husband.

claver: *clover*
bield: *shelter*
shiel: *bothy, shelter*
eild: *visage*
cannie wale: *wise choice*
routhie: *plentiful, abundant*
craps and kye: *crops and cattle*
buskie: *bosky, wooded.*
faught: *fight*
canniest gate: *wisest path*
ay fu' han't is fechtin best: *always full handed gives you the best chance*
unco: *extreme (in this context)*
yill: *ale*
gear: *possessions*
gowd and siller: *gold and silver*

'Bonie Jean'.

A Red, Red Rose

O my Luve's like a red, red rose
That's newly sprung in June;
O my Luve's like the melody
That's sweetly played in tune.

So fair art thou, my bonie lass,
So deep in luve am I;
And I will luve thee still, my dear,
Till a' the seas gang dry.

Till a' the seas gang dry, my dear,
And the rocks melt wi' the sun;
And I will love thee still, my dear,
While the sands o' life shall run.

And fare-thee-weel, my only Luve!
And fare-thee-weel awhile!
And I will come again, my Luve,
Tho' 'twere ten thousand mile.

Tune: Major Graham by Niel Gow

Although there is no mention of Jean by name in this, one of the poet's best-known songs, there is something about the timeless affection evoked here, coupled with the simplicity of the words, that reminds me of Burns's love for his wife. The 'sands o' life' section echoes the last, moving verse of *O, Were I On Parnassus Hill*, with its evocation of enduring love; while the theme of parting and reunion recalls the couple's chequered early relationship. The description of the lass as a 'red, red rose' seems peculiarly apt for Jean, who was a striking brunette, with vivid colouring. The original melody that the poet intended for this song (not the rather pedestrian tune that is so frequently sung) is incredibly joyful, with soaring notes that surely must have suited Jean's unique 'wood-note wild'.

Penny Wedding, after an 1818 painting
by David Wilkie.

Letters

Mauchline scene, near the castle.

Extracts From Robert Burns's Correspondence about and to Jean Armour

The dramatic progress of Robert Burns's relationship with Jean Armour, his wife and his muse, can be followed through many of the poet's letters, as well as his poems. Burns was such a prolific correspondent that one wonders how he found time for everything else in his busy life (not least, the creation of a huge body of poetry and song).

A peculiarly mercurial character emerges from these letters. Burns had a tendency to suit the tone of his correspondence to the character of the recipient, so he can be forthright and occasionally brash to male friends; mischievous and a little coy when writing to female contemporaries; careful and grave in his correspondence with the older, wiser Frances Dunlop; and – in the scant handful of letters to her that survive – loving and casually 'domestic' when writing to Jean.

These extracts begin around the time of Jean's first pregnancy. The couple had agreed to marry. Jean's horrified father banished his daughter to relatives in Paisley, and prevailed upon Mr Aiken, an Ayr lawyer, to cut the names out of the 'marriage agreement' that the poet had prudently drawn up for Jean and himself to sign. It is probable that this had no effect on the legitimacy of the union, but the Armours disliked Burns at this time and were prepared to try any measure to part the couple. Somewhat unfairly, Burns blamed Jean for submitting to what must have been intense family pressure.

Mossgiel, late 1785.
To John Arnot, an early subscriber to the first volume of poetry

I have lost, sir, that dearest earthly treasure, that greatest blessing here below, that last, best gift which compleated Adam's happiness in the garden of bliss, I have lost – I have lost – my trembling hand refuses its office, the frightened ink recoils up the quill ... I have lost – a – a – A WIFE! ... There is a pretty large portion of bedlam in the composition of a Poet at any time; but on this occasion, I was nine parts and nine tenths out of ten, stark, staring mad.

But this is not all. Already the holy beagles, the houghmagandie pack begin to snuff the scent; and I expect every moment to see them cast off, and hear them after me in full cry: but as I am an old fox, I shall give them dodging and doubling for it and bye and bye I intend to earth among the mountains of Jamaica.

The 'houghmagandie pack' was the 'fornication police' – the Mauchline kirk elders who were charged with monitoring the morals of the townspeople. Some of them took this very seriously indeed, although it is obvious from parish records that the main aim of the 'holy beagles' was to protect women from being abandoned in pregnancy (such women would – it has to be acknowledged – become a drain on parish funds).

Mossgiel, 15th April 1786.
To his friend and landlord Gavin Hamilton

Old Mr Armour prevailed with him [*Mr Aiken, the lawyer from Ayr, who was also a friend of the poet*] to mutilate that unlucky paper, yesterday – Would you believe it? – tho I had not a hope, nor even a wish, to make her mine after her conduct, yet when he told me the names were all cut out of the paper, my heart died within me, and he cut my very veins with the news. Perdition seize her falsehood, and perjurious perfidy! But God bless her and forgive my poor, once-dear, misguided girl. She is ill advised. Do not despise me, Sir: I am indeed a fool, but a knave is an infinitely worse character than anybody, I hope, will dare to give, the unfortunate Robert Burns.

A clearly pregnant Jean came back to Mauchline from Paisley in June 1786. By this time, Burns was courting Highland Mary and planning to leave Scotland for Jamaica. But he was also planning to publish a volume of his poems, funded by subscription.

Mossgiel, 12th June 1786.
To his friend David Brice

Poor, ill advised, ungrateful Armour came home on Friday last. You have heard all the particulars of that affair and a black affair it is. What she thinks of her conduct now, I don't know. One thing I know, she has made me compleatly miserable. Never man lov'd or rather ador'd a woman more than I did her and, to confess a truth between you and me, I do still love her to distraction after all, tho' I won't tell her so, tho' I see her, which I don't want to do. My poor dear, unfortunate Jean! How happy have I been in her arms! It is not the losing her that makes me so unhappy, but for *her* sake I feel most severely. I foresee she is on the road to, I am afraid, eternal ruin; and those who made so much noise, and showed so much grief, at the thought of her being my wife, may, some day, see her connected in such a manner as may give them more real cause of vexation. I am sure I do not wish it: may Almighty God forgive her! ... I have tryed often to forget her; I have run into all kinds of dissipation and riot, Mason-meetings, drinking matches, and other mischief, to drive her out of my head, but all in vain; and now for a grand cure, the Ship is on her way home that is to take me out to Jamaica, and then, farewell dear old Scotland, and farewell, dear, ungrateful Jean, for never, never will I see you more!

Mossgiel, 9th July 1786.
To his friend John Richmond

I have waited on Armour since her return home, not ... from any the least view of reconciliation, but merely to ask for her health; and – to you I will confess it – from a foolish hankering fondness, very ill placed indeed. The Mother forbade me the house; nor did Jean shew that penitence that might have been expected.

Mossgiel, 17th July 1786.
To his friend David Brice

Poor, foolish Armour is come back again to Mauchline, and I went to call for her and her mother forbade me the house; nor did she herself express much sorrow for what she has done. I have already appeared publickly in Church, and was indulged in the liberty of standing in my own seat ... Jean and her friends insisted much that she should stand along with me in the kirk but the minister would not allow it, which bred a great trouble, I assure you, and I am blamed as the cause of it, tho I am sure I am innocent.

'Friends', in this context, generally means family. It is doubtful that a heavily pregnant Jean wanted to stand up in the kirk as an admission of her sins, although her parents and the elders, Holy Willie Fisher among them, may have wished it. The minister, Mr Auld, who emerges as a stern but kindly man, allowed her to send a letter of apology instead. This was copied into the Kirk Session Minutes book and signed by Jean.

Old Rome Foord, Kilmarnock, 30th July 1786. To his friend John Richmond

Would you believe it? Armour has got a warrant to throw me in jail till I find security for an enormous sum. This they keep an entire secret, but I got it by a channel they little dream of, and I am wandering from one friend's house to another, and like a true son of the Gospel 'have nowhere to lay my head'. I know you will pour an execration on her head, but spare the poor, ill advised Girl for my sake, though may all the Furies that rend the injured, enraged Lover's bosom await the old harridan, her Mother, until her latest hour! May Hell string the arm of Death to throw the fatal dart, and all the winds of warring elements rouse the infernal flames to welcome her approach. For heaven's sake burn this letter and never show it to a living creature. I write it in a moment of rage, reflecting on my miserable situation – exiled, abandon'd and forlorn.

Burns had taken refuge with his mother's cousin at Old Rome, outside Kilmarnock, not far from Mauchline. We can probably assume that the 'channel they little dream of' was Jean herself. Burns's first volume of poems was issued by John Wilson of Kilmarnock on the day after this letter was written.

* Old Rome Foord, Kilmarnock, 1st August 1786.
To his friend James Smith

> O Jeany, thou hast stolen away my soul!
> In vain I strive against the lov'd idea:
> Thy tender image sallies on my thoughts,
> My firm resolves become an easy prey.

Against two things however, I am fix'd as Fate: staying at home and owning her conjugally. The first, by Heaven, I will not do! The last, by Hell I will never do!

... If you see Jean tell her, I will meet her, so help me Heaven in my hour of need!

* This is the probable location.

Mossgiel, 3rd September 1786.
To his friend John Richmond

Wish me luck, dear Richmond. Armour has just now brought me a fine boy and girl at one throw. God bless them, poor little dears!

The twins were named Robert and Jean after their parents. Once weaned, the little boy went to the Burns family farm at Mossgiel, just outside the town, while the girl stayed in the Armour household in the Cowgate, Mauchline. Burns didn't go to Jamaica and poor Highland Mary died of typhus in Greenock, although since she had agreed to take up a position as a nursemaid in Glasgow, we might wonder whether she ever expected the poet to join her. Perhaps he had promised to send for her from the Indies. Burns himself was already reaping the rewards of his sudden celebrity in Edinburgh, returning occasionally to visit his family.

Mauchline, 11th June 1787.
To his friend James Smith

I date this from Mauchline, where I arrived on Friday even last. I slept at John Dows, and called for my daughter. ... If anything had been wanting to disgust me compleatly at Armour's family, their mean servile compliance would have done it.

John Dow's was a respectable inn, very close to the Armour house on the Cowgate. Burns had become a great success in the capital, and Jean's parents were clearly changing their minds about his prospects as a son-in-law.

Edinburgh, 25th October 1787.
To his friend John Richmond

By the way, I hear I am a girl out of pocket and by careless murdering mischance too, which has provoked me and vexed me a good deal. I beg you will write me by post immediately on receipt of this, and let me know the news of Armour's family, if the world begin to talk of Jean's appearance in any way.

This is the only reference to the untimely and presumably accidental death of Jean and Robert's little girl, aged some 13 months. The reference to 'Jean's appearance' indicates that Jean had fallen pregnant some time during the summer of 1787 and was again carrying the poet's twins.

Mossgiel, 23rd February 1788.
To Agnes McLehose, aka 'Clarinda'

Now for a little news that will please you. I, this morning, as I came home, called for a certain woman. I am disgusted with her; I cannot endure her! I, while my heart smote me for the prophanity, tried to compare her with my Clarinda: 'twas setting the expiring glimmer of a farthing taper beside the cloudless glory of the meridian sun. Here was tasteless insipidity, vulgarity of soul and mercenary fawning, there, polished good sense, heaven born genius and the most generous, the most delicate, the most tender Passion. I have done with her and she with me.

The affair with 'Clarinda' was mostly conducted by an overheated correspondence. Nancy McLehose was married, albeit estranged from her reputedly cruel husband. She clearly adored Burns, and obviously desired him, but her religious and social scruples were overwhelming. There is no evidence that the relationship was ever fully consummated, and much of the correspondence reads – to female eyes anyway – like a prolonged but ultimately unsuccessful attempt to get Nancy into his bed. Whatever the truth of the matter, it produced some of the most beautiful songs the poet ever wrote.

It's clear from the above extract that Nancy had expressed a certain jealousy of Jean. Noting the successive dates of the above, and the notorious 'horse litter' letter below, gives us some insight into the turmoil of Burns's emotions at this time. We should remember that Jean had lost her daughter only four or five months previously, and was once again pregnant. The 'mercenary fawning' he so affects to despise probably originated in utter despair. Probably too, he knew it.

Mauchline, 3rd March 1788.
To his friend Robert Ainslie

Jean, I found banished like a martyr – forlorn, destitute and friendless; all for the good old cause. I have reconciled her to her fate, and I have reconciled her to her mother. I have taken her a room. I have taken her to my arms. I have given her a mahogany bed. I have given her a guinea ... But, as I always am on every occasion, I have been prudent and cautious to an astonishing degree. I swore her privately and solemnly never to attempt any claim on me as a husband, even though anybody should persuade her she had such a claim (which she had not) neither during my life nor after my death. She did all this like a good girl and I took the opportunity of some dry horse litter and gave her such a thundering scalade that electrified the very marrow of her bones.

The graphic Ainslie letter is one of the most difficult for biographers and novelists to deal with. Jean was heavily pregnant when the 'horse litter' scene – shocking in its implied brutality – took place. The second set of twins was born prematurely only a little while after, and did not survive.

The letter reads like a braggardly and not very successful attempt to rationalise sensations of guilt over what – to modern sensibilities – sounds very like an assault, or at least a sexual encounter in which one partner was compliant but markedly less enthusiastic than the other. These were, of course, different times, with different codes of conduct. Nevertheless, it proved to be a turning point in the relationship, a volte-face that may have been prompted by Burns's abiding love and pity for Jean and his recognition that, according to his own moral code of kindliness, he had behaved very badly indeed. Whatever the truth of their feelings for one another – and only those most closely involved knew for sure – the couple were officially married very soon after.

Mauchline, 28th April 1788.
To his friend James Smith

...there is, you must know, a certain clean-lim'd, handsome, bewitching young Hussy of your acquaintance to whom I have lately and privately given a matrimonial title to my Corpus. ... Now for business – I intend to present Mrs Burns with a printed shawl, an article of which I dare say you have a variety, 'tis my first present to her since I have irrevocably called her mine, and I have a kind of whimsical wish to get her the said first present from an old and much valued friend of hers and mine.

James Smith had moved to Linlithgow, where he had gone into partnership with a calico printer. 'Clean', in this context, means finely made.

Mauchline, April 1788.
To Margaret Chalmers

Shortly after my last return to Ayrshire, I married 'my Jean'. This was not in consequence of the attachment of romance perhaps but I had a long and much-loved fellow creature's happiness or misery in my determination and I durst not trifle with so important a deposit. Nor have I any cause to repent it. If I have not got polite tattle, modish manners, and fashionable dress, I am not sickened and disgusted with the multiform curse of boarding-school affectation, and I have got the handsomest figure, the sweetest temper, the soundest constitution and the kindest heart in the country. Mrs Burns believes, as firmly as her creed, that I am *le plus bel esprit, et le plus honnete homme* in the universe, although she scarcely ever in her life, except the Scriptures ... spent five minutes together on either prose or verse. I must except also from this last, a certain late publication of Scots poems, which she has perused very devoutly; and all the ballads in the country, as she has (Oh the partial lover, you will cry) the finest 'wood note wild' I have ever heard. ... She is still at Mauchline, as I am building my house, for this hovel that I shelter in while occasionally here, is pervious to every blast that blows, and every shower that falls, and I am only preserved from being chilled to death by being suffocated with smoke.

> Burns distinguishes between an attachment of 'romance' and one of love, a distinction that even today shouldn't be too hard to understand. His frequent reference to 'much lov'd' with regard to Jean in his correspondence seems significant. Love invariably outranked romance where Burns was concerned.

Ellisland, 13th June 1788.
To Mrs Frances Dunlop, friend and frequent correspondent

I must inform you, Madam, that ... I am indeed A HUSBAND. ... I found a once much-lov'd and still much lov'd female, literally and truly cast out to the mercy of the naked elements, but I enabled her to purchase a shelter; and there is no sporting with a creature's happiness or misery. The most placid good-nature and sweetness of disposition, a warm heart, gratefully devoted with its powers to love one; vigorous health and sprightly chearfulness, set off to best advantage by a more than common handsome figure; these, I think in a woman, may make a tolerable good wife, though she should never have read a page but The Scriptures of the Old and New Testament, nor have 'danced in a brighter Assembly than a Penny-pay Wedding.'

When Jean fell pregnant for the second time, she was not 'cast out' as literally as Burns asserted. She certainly took shelter at Willie's Mill, near Tarbolton, and kindly Willie Muir, the miller, had been a friend of the poet's late father, but he was also a friend of the Armour family. One version of the story is that Jean was visiting Willie's Mill when her family sent word that it would be better if she should stay there, perhaps in an effort to avoid the inevitable gossip in the town.

Surprisingly, there is no mention of this second pregnancy in the Kirk Session Minutes until after the babies are born, so perhaps the strategy worked. A 'Penny-pay Wedding' was a celebration where the guests contributed to the cost of the feast. This custom continued well into the twentieth century in Ayrshire.

Mauchline, 18th July 1788.
To Peter Hill, of Creech's bookshop in Edinburgh

From Ellisland in Nithsdale to Mauchline in Kyle, is forty and five miles; there, a house a-building and farm inclosures and improvements to tend; here, a new – not so much indeed a new as a *young* wife. Good God, sir, could my dearest brother expect a regular correspondence from me!

There is some evidence that Burns did indeed neglect his new Ellisland farm a little, spending as much time as he could with Jean in Mauchline. He himself happily refers to this period as 'the Honeymoon'.

Mauchline, 10th August 1788.
To Mrs Frances Dunlop, friend and frequent correspondent

Mrs Burns, Madam, is the identical woman who was the mother of twice twins to me in seventeen months. When she first found herself 'As women wish to be who love their Lords' as I lov'd her near to distraction, I took some previous steps to a private marriage. Her Parents got the hint; and in detestation of my guilt of being a poor devil, not only forbade me her company and their house, but on my rumoured West Indian voyage, got a warrant to incarcerate me in jail till I should find security in my about-to-be Paternal relation. You know my lucky reverse of fortune. On my eclatant return to Mauchline, I was made very welcome to visit my girl. The usual consequences began to betray her; and as I was at that time laid up a cripple in Edinburgh, she was turned, literally turned out of doors, and I wrote to a friend to shelter her, till my return. I was not under the least verbal obligation to her, but her happiness or misery were in my hands and who could trifle with such a deposit? To the least temptation of jealousy or Infidelity, I am an equal stranger. My preservative from the first is the most thorough consciousness of her sentiments of honour, and her attachment to me; my antidote against the last is my long and deep-rooted affection for her.

Ellisland, 12th September 1788.
To Jean Armour

My dear Love, I received your kind letter with a pleasure which no letter but one from you could have given me. I dreamed of you the whole night last, but alas! I fear it will be three weeks yet, ere I can hope for the happiness of seeing you. My harvest is going on. I have some to cut down still, but I put in two stacks today, so I am as tired as a dog.

You might get one of Gilbert's sweet milk cheeses [*two or three words torn away*] and send it to [*letter torn here*]

On second thoughts, I believe you had best get the half of Gilbert's web of table-linen and make it up; tho I think it damnable dear, but it is no out-laid money to us you know. I have just now consulted my old Landlady about table-linen and she thinks I may have the best for two shillings per yard; so after all, let it alone until I return and some day soon I will be in Dumfries, and will ask the prices there. I expect your new gowns will be very forward, or ready to make, against I be home to get the Baeveridge. I have written my long-thought-on letter to Mr Graham, the Commissioner of Excise, and have sent him a sheetful of poetry besides. Now I talk of poetry, I had a fine Strathspey among my hands to make verses to, for Johnson's Collection which I [*remainder of letter missing*]

'Baeveridge' is usually, in this context, a drink to seal a bargain, perhaps here with the dressmaker.

This letter is one of the few indications – although there are others, in the poet's notes to the various songs – that Burns involved his wife in discussions about songs and suitable melodies. One feels that there may have been other letters to Jean that did not survive. Even those that exist seem to have been treated more carelessly than his other correspondence.

Ellisland, 14th October 1788.
To Jean Armour

My dearest Love, You need not come on Sunday to meet me on the road, for I am engaged that day to dine with Mr Logan at Laycht, so it will be in the evening before I arrive at Mauchline.

You must get ready for Nithsdale as fast as possible, for I have an offer of a house in the very neibourhood with some furniture in it, all of which I shall have the use of for nothing till my own house be got ready; and I am determined to remove you from Ayrshire immediately, as I am a sufferer by not being on the farm myself. We will want a Maid servant of consequence: if you can hear of any to hire, ask after them. The apples are all sold and gone. I am extremely happy at the idea of your coming to Nithsdale, as it will save us from these cruel separations. The house is one in which a Mr Newal lived during the summer, who is gone to Dumfries in Winter. It is a large house, but we will only occupy a room or two of it.

Ellisland, 9th February 1789.
To his cousin James Burness

After I parted from you, for many months, my life was one continued scene of dissipation. Here, at last, I am become stationary and have taken a farm and – a wife. The farm lies beautifully situated on the banks of the Nith, a large river than runs by Dumfries and falls into the Solway Firth. I have gotten a lease of my farm as long as I pleased; but how it may turn out is just a guess, as it is yet to improve and inclose etc; however I have good hopes of my bargain on the whole.

My wife is my Jean, with whose story you are partly acquainted. I found I had a much loved fellow creature's happiness or misery among my hands, and I durst not trifle with so sacred a deposit. Indeed, I have not any reason to repent the step I have taken, as I have attached myself to a very good wife, and have shaken myself loose of a very bad failing.

Edinburgh, 20th February 1789.
To Jean Armour

I cannot precisely say when I will leave this town, my dearest friend, but at farthest, I think I will be with you on Sunday come eight days, perhaps sooner. I had a horrid journey ... [*three lines missing*]

I have settled matters greatly to my satisfaction with Mr Creech. He is certainly not what he should be, nor has he given me what I should have, but I am better than I expected. Farewell! I long much to see you – God bless you!

Ellisland, 11th April 1791.
To Mrs Frances Dunlop, friend and correspondent

... life is chequered, joy and sorrow, for on Saturday morning last Mrs Burns made me a present of a fine boy, rather stouter but not so handsome as your God-son at his time of life was [*the godson in question was Francis Wallace Burns, born in 1789*]. Indeed I look on your little Namesake to be my *chef d'oeuvre* in that species of manufacture, as I look on Tam o' Shanter to be my standard performance in the Poetical line. 'Tis true, both the one and the other discover a spice of roguish waggery that might perhaps be as well spared, but then they also shew in my opinion a force of genius and a finishing polish that I despair of ever excelling. Mrs Burns is getting stout again and laid as lustily about her today at breakfast as a Reaper from the cornridge. That is the peculiar privilege and blessing of our hale, sprightly damsels, that are bred among hay and heather. We cannot hope for that highly polished mind, that charming delicacy of soul which is found among the Female world in the more elevated stations of life ...

Accounts from visitors to the household speak of finding Jean in floods of tears, and we can assume that poor post-partum Jean, with a baby at the breast again, was not quite so happy with her lot as Burns portrays here.

Ann Park, the barmaid at the Globe Inn in Dumfries, had given birth to Burns's daughter, Elizabeth, on 31st March, in Leith. In 1793, when Ann decided that she no longer wanted the child, Jean took her in and brought her up alongside her own children.

Brow Well, on the Solway, 10th July 1796. To Gilbert Burns, his younger brother

It will be no very pleasing news to you to be told that I am dangerously ill and not likely to get better. An inveterate rheumatism has reduced me to such a state of debility, and my appetite is gone, so that I can scarce stand on my legs. I have been a week at sea bathing, and I will continue there or in a friend's house in the country all the summer. God help my wife and children if I am taken from their head! They will be poor indeed. I have contracted one or two serious debts, partly from my illness these many months and partly from too much thoughtlessness as to expense when I came to town that will cut in too much on the little I leave them in your hand.

There has been plenty of speculation about the poet's final illness, but the most likely cause seems to have been acute endocarditis, or inflammation of the heart muscle, which would cause all his reported symptoms, and would be fatal. It's known that he suffered from severe toothache some little while before his final illness, and an infection such as this might be enough to trigger an acute phase of a chronic condition. Sea bathing would not have helped.

Brow Well, on the Solway, 10th July 1796. To James Armour, his father-in-law

For Heaven's sake and as you value the welfare of your daughter and my wife, do, my dearest Sir, write to Fife to Mrs Armour to come if possible. My wife thinks she can yet reckon upon a fortnight. The medical people order me as I value my existence to fly to seabathing and country quarters, so it is ten thousand chances to one that I shall not be within a dozen miles of her when her hour comes. What situation for her, poor girl, without a single friend by her on such a serious moment.

I have now been a week at salt water and though I think I have got some good by it, yet I have some secret fears that this business will be dangerous if not fatal.

Jean was heavily pregnant again at this time and would have needed her mother to assist with the birth. Burns had been on good terms with Jean's father for some years, but Mrs Armour was visiting relatives in Fife, and communications would have been slow.

Brow Well, on the Solway, 14th July 1796.
To Jean Armour

My dearest love, I delayed writing until I could tell you what effect sea-bathing was likely to produce. It would be injustice to deny that it has eased my pains, and, I think, has strengthened me, but my appetite is still extremely bad. No flesh nor fish can I swallow; porridge and milk are the only thing I can taste. I am very happy to hear, by Miss Jess Lewars, that you are all well. My very best and kindest compliments to her, and to all the children. I will see you on Sunday. Your affectionate husband, R.B.

Dumfries, 18th July 1796.
To James Armour, his father-in-law

My dear Sir, Do, for heaven's sake, send Mrs Armour here immediately. My wife is hourly expecting to be put to bed. Good God! What a situation for her to be in, poor girl, without a friend! I returned from sea-bathing quarters today, and my medical friends would almost persuade me that I am better, but I think and feel that my strength is so gone that the disorder will prove fatal to me.

> Burns died in his house in Dumfries on the morning of 21st July 1796, at the age of thirty-seven. Jean gave birth to his last son, Maxwell, on 25th July, the day of his funeral.

Acknowledgements

Thanks are due to the many individuals and institutions that have helped me while I was researching *The Jewel* and this companion volume of poems, songs and letters. A full list and bibliography can be found in *The Jewel*, but I should single out Creative Scotland, the Burns Birthplace Museum in Alloway, Burns House Museum in Mauchline, Ellisland Farm and The National Library of Scotland.

The poems, pictures and letters are from my own nineteenth-century collections of the works of Robert Burns, but *The Complete Letters of Robert Burns*, edited by James A Mackay, was invaluable in checking chronology and accuracy. The notes are my own.

Grateful thanks as ever to Sara Hunt and Craig Hillsley of Saraband, for their expertise, hard work and generous support.

Finally, I would like to dedicate this volume to the late Stewart Forson Sanderson, Scottish folklorist and linguist, who supervised my postgraduate Masters degree at Leeds University where he was Director of the Institute of Dialect and Folk Life Studies (later Chairman of the School of English). His guidance gave me a good grounding in all aspects of Folk Life Studies, and his wise supervision has influenced and informed my research as a historical novelist ever since.

Catherine Czerkawska